Buttermilk Book Publishing

Myrtle Beach, South Carolina

Copyright T. Allen Winn 2022

All Rights Reserved

This book is an account of the forming of the band The Horry Counter Pickers as conducted through interviews with the trio of Pickers reminiscing about the start and shared love for pickin'.

Typecast in Times New Roman

ISBN 978-1-7365555-8-3

Definition: Picker

A person who plays a plucked instrument, especially a guitar, banjo, or mandolin.

Definition: Bluegrass

A kind of country music influenced by jazz and blues and characterized by virtuosic playing of banjos and guitars and high pitched, close harmony vocals.

Picking The Pickers

From left to right (Danny Singleton, Doug Bell, Ron Walker)

The Horry County Pickers consists of three pickers, Ron Walker, Danny Singleton and Doug Bell. The trio's connecting was not exactly planned but might have been destiny's choice instead. Ron Walker needed a sawblade and asked friend Gene Singleton if he knew where he could put his hands on one. He and Gene had become friends at Carolina Forest High School where Gene's son, Winn, and Ron's daughter, Lexi performed in the Carolina Forest Show Choir. Gene told Ron that his brother Danny probably had the type of sawblade because he had just about everything. Gene contacted him and indeed he did. Danny Singleton immediately took the sawblade to Ron's house where he was having a yard sale at the time. To thank Danny for coming through for him, and after discovering that Danny was an avid reader, Ron gave Danny a bunch of books that had belonged to his wife, Trish's father who was a professor a WVU. Later, once he got to know Danny, Ron realized that beyond being an avid reader, he was a man with a wealth of knowledge. He was amazed by how Danny could take a complex situation, think on it and come up with a solution to solve whatever problem needed solving. Danny possessed the ability to go far beyond how things worked, almost down to a theory on how something worked like it did. The two swapped stories about picking with it ending in Ron tossing out an invite for him to drop by sometime and pick. Danny took him up on the offer and they began picking on occasions in Ron's living room. Their friendship blossomed, the two finding common ground in their playing.

Doug Bell knew Ron as a coworker at Coastal Carolina University. Doug was employed at Coastal Carolina University for about twenty-five years as a proofer and editor. Ron began telling him about Danny and how Danny loved Ralph Stanley and the old time music. Doug had never met Danny, but his gut told him the two would get along just fine. Ron invited Doug to join their little impromptu gatherings. Through conversations during their sessions Danny and Doug found that they shared something in common. Both belonged to families that had resided in the area since the early 1700s. Finding common ground, they enjoyed talking history. Doug had played the guitar since he was twenty years old but was thirty-nine when he bought his mandolin. They began practicing and enjoying every minute of it. Their journey in picking as a group began in 2013.

Ron said there were two people in life that angered him because of their natural ability to pick up an instrument and play it: Doug and Danny. Ron said his approach was more of a struggle, having to think about it. He laughed, adding to this day he thought he was the only one of the three with a music book. He added that it isn't because he forgets it, he just wants reminders of what's in the songs. He confessed he does not read music. Doug took piano and can read music but said when playing, he could not differentiate A, B, C, D on the mandolin. He plays completely by ear. The three pickers had this in common. Ron explained the chords used to play Bluegrass, adding that Danny could play all of them flawlessly.

Ron reminisced about how awesome it was and how far they had come since those pickin' sessions in his living room. None of them had ever been involved in a band nor had performed in public. Their typical audience had been just themselvies or maybe a cat or dog as their captive audience. Ron recorded the trio's sessions and photographed them in what he described as a tiny office (living room) with not enough room for them to squirt or sneeze, elbow to elbow with three instruments. Danny's favorite song to play was *Angel Band* and it was the first song they played as a group. Doug designed a lead in and a break for the song and, to this day, they still play it the same way.

Now for the question inquiring minds might seek; the origin of the name 'The Horry County Pickers.' Ron confessed it was his idea even though he was the only one of them that did not originally grow up in Horry County. Doug and Danny were homegrown. Ron overheard Danny and Doug talking about family and their wealth of family history. Almost everywhere they performed. Doug or Danny would point to someone saying they knew the person, or they thought they were related to them. It just seemed logical that Horry County be included in the name. And after all, they were pickers. It seemed the perfect name. Ron, being artistic, had to visually put it into a logo.

But wait, as the info commercial goes. There is more. The Pickers were almost named something else. Doug explained the backdrop. About a hundred years ago, back in 1921, five members of the Bigham family of Pamplico, South Carolina were killed. This resulted in a sensational trial that was covered nationwide. There have been generations of killings related to the Bigham family. In 1924 there was another murder trial held in Conway. The Bighams were involved yet again. There was a book published titled *The Last of the Bighams*. Someone who worked with Doug and Ron at CCU suggested that they call their band 'The Last of the Bighams.' Obviously, many people would not get it. A lot of the older locals probably would.

Ron also had another thought. He was a fan of the group 'Asleep at the Wheel' formed by Ray Benson. He had thought it would be hilarious to name the band 'Ronny Ray and the Rangers'. Ron had made a poster of 'Asleep at the Wheel' and had superimposed their faces on the musicians, posting it on his office door for a spell. Everyone had nicknames like Ranger Doug.

The first public performance by The Horry County Pickers was at Conway Manor, an assisted living facility. The Pickers had never intended to play for anybody but area nursing homes. They shared a love for the elderly community. Doug confessed again that he had never intended to play in public and until he hooked up with Ron and Danny, had not realized that he had been playing rhythm completely wrong. You do it on the two and the four count and not on the one and the two count, as he had been playing. He had been chopping it wrong. Ron admitted it was the blind leading the blind because he had never played bluegrass. He had grown up playing R&B and the 70's music of the Eagles. Doug had not played bluegrass either, focusing more on what is known as 'old time music.'

Doug explained that 'old time music' was a bit of a different genre from bluegrass. The first country music was family string bands like the Carters. Bluegrass began when Bill Monroe met Earl Scruggs in 1946. The combination of those two made bluegrass. Doug expanded, saying old time music is a cross between folk music and hymns with ballads. So, one might wonder what may have drawn the trio to bluegrass. Obviously, it was not Doug or Ron's music of choice. They credit

Danny as being the only true picker in the group. Ron said he was a rhythm guitar player and Doug could pick. Ron considered Danny the bluegrass expert and the inspiration for the pickers. He set the tempo for their playing. Doug was always a true fan of Bill Monroe and Danny lived and breathed it too. He credits Danny with knowing the old, the new, and everything in between. He added that Danny's favorite group was the Stanley Brothers. Ron's uncles played 'Americana' at family reunions, so he was not exposed to bluegrass.

While their performances seemed a mixed bag, Danny preferred for them to not stray far from bluegrass. Ron confessed that he had gotten into trouble many times with Danny for stretching out and playing other genres instead of strictly bluegrass. That resulted in Danny refusing to talk with him for weeks. He finally reconciled their differences when Ron asked him to do a pickin' practice session. Danny agreed provided Ron promised not to play any of that other music. Doug took sides with Danny. Danny is considered the group's founding father even though the original invites to play were tossed out by Ron. After they had played a few times as a group, Danny confided to Doug that he really liked their sound. It was something he always wanted to be part of.

As stated, none of them had ever played in public. Doug added that he never considered playing in public. Ditto, added Ron, but he did push Danny to do it. They eventually convinced Doug. Danny embraced the opportunity after realizing the sound was heading in a good direction. He gained confidence and eventually made his own confession, telling Ron that he was the only reason for him playing in public. Danny became deeply involved in the journey, admitting to Doug that he had experienced drinking problems in his past. He credited music with helping him overcome his addiction. Danny would put on a record and play while listening to the music. It served as the perfect therapy.

Doug never utilized this approach. He would listen to the record and then turn it off before playing what he had heard. He could not tune his guitar to the correct pitch to play along with a record. Everyone has their quirks. Doug did it his way back then with no one around to influence him musically. The three journeymen followed their own paths. Who could have visualized where these paths would lead?

The Horry County Pickers had discovered their calling and embraced the passion for pickin' as a trio. Performing for nursing homes and assisted living facilities remained their primary focus. They eventually eased into playing at other venues. Make no mistake, they never forgot their roots. The elderly deserved their attention and fellowship. Nothing made them happier than entertaining those forgotten folks that some seemingly tossed away. The smiles and joy on the faces of those at the homes and facilities were priceless. The Pickers are givers and forever community driven.

(Danny Singleton, Ron Walker, Doug Bell)

Ron Walker Journey

This is Ron Walker's journey to becoming the catalyst for encouraging the pickers to pick at his home back in 2013, a pickin' jam session of sorts. Part of this interview was conducted Christmas Eve 2015 at the author's home in Myrtle Beach and an additional interview occurred June 28, 2022, same location.

Ron: "I think my first musical influence was a takeaway from family reunions when I was just a kid. Once a year my family would get together and we're talking about real homestyle family reunions. I had my beginning in San Antonio, Texas, being raised there for the first segment of my life."

San Antonio straddles South Texas and Central Texas and is on the southwestern corner of an urban mega-region known as the Texas Triangle. A megalopolis in laymen terms is typically defined as a chain of roughly adjacent metropolitan areas. Factual tidbits about Ron's birthplace: San Antonio was named for Saint Anthony of Padua, whose feast day is on June 13, by a 1691 Spanish expedition in the area. The city contains five 18th-century Spanish frontier missions, including The Alamo and San Antonio Missions National Historical Park, which were designated UNESCO World Heritage Sites in 2015.

Following the Civil War, San Antonio prospered as a center of the cattle industry, remaining a frontier city, with a mixture of cultures that was different from other US cities during this period. At the beginning of the 20th century, the streets of the city's downtown were widened to accommodate street cars and modern traffic. At that time, many of the older historic buildings were demolished in the process of this modernization.

Ron: "My father retired from the Air Force. We then moved near Muscle Shoals, Alabama. One of the pluses of him retiring was, that as a kid, I would get to go to a lot of the events we had previously missed out on in Texas. Unfortunately, because we now lived twelve hours away in Alabama, we couldn't just load up the car and drive twelve hours to attend the family reunions. This was the price we paid for leaving San Antonio in our rearview mirror. We did manage to get home for Christmas, family being an important part of my growing up.

My immediate family consisted of a brother and a sister. On my mom's side of the family were five kids and on my dad's side there were eight. My grandfather was Dewy Monroe Vanderbilt, and he was married to

Gladys Ann Talbert. I remember vividly my Uncle James. Then there was Uncle Howard, Uncle Everett Dewey Monroe Vandiver, Jr. that went by Uncle Junior. The Walkers from my dad's side originated from Scotland and the Vandiver's were Pennsylvania Dutch. I'm not sure what Pennsylvania Dutch are. It is an interesting mix for sure."

Interesting fact indeed and somewhat of a clarification that the head picker is not actually of Dutch descent: The Pennsylvania Dutch are a cultural group formed by early German-speaking immigrants to Pennsylvania and their descendants. This early wave of settlers, which would eventually coalesce to form the Pennsylvania Dutch, began in the late 17th century and concluded in the late 18th century. Most of these immigrants originated in what is today southwestern Germany, i.e., Rhineland-Palatinate and Baden-Württemberg; other prominent groups were Alsatians, Dutch, French Huguenots (French Protestants), Moravians from Bohemia and Moravia, and Swiss. Historically they spoke the dialect of German known as Pennsylvania German or Pennsylvania Dutch. In this context, the word "Dutch" does not refer to the Dutch people (Netherlanders) or their descendants, but to Deitsch or Deutsch (German). The Pennsylvania Dutch are people of various religious affiliations, most of them Lutheran or Reformed, but many Anabaptists as well.

Ron: "I never actually met my grandfather. He was shot in the back in 1938 by a common crook that murdered him to steal his money. This was during the depression years, a time when it was tough to find work, specifically in the area where he lived. He had to go to Peoria, Illinois to find work where he was employed at the Caterpillar factory. He was walking home one night after work and was ambushed from behind. He died of that gunshot wound and his murderer was never found and brought to justice. This left my grandmother with eight kids to raise, not an easy task in any given situation, especially back then. My dad is second to the oldest. He had a sister, Shirley, who was his oldest sibling. My dad's way out of this after his dad was murdered was to go into the service, enlisting in the Air Force. He was underage and lied about his age as many kids did. He was just seventeen. He and his cousin, Herman Mitchell went in on the buddy system which was supposed to guarantee that those entering under this system were stationed at same location and served their time together.

They arrived at the camp and departed on a bus where the officers in charge lined them all up in some semblance of formation. The officer said, 'Everybody on the buddy system raise your hands.' Of course, Dad and Mitchell were two of many that had enlisted under this premise. The officer then said, 'Say goodbye to your buddies.' Dad and Mitchell never saw each other again for three years. So much for a buddy system and an enlistment promise. This really wasn't a very good buddy system, now, was it?"

In the relatively innocent and emotionally charged days of the 1940's, soldiers and sailors were encouraged to form close bonds with their fellow troops. They needed to trust and count on each other. Their lives depended on it. Most of these young men were just entering manhood. Many came from landlocked states and small towns and farms. They didn't know the wicked ways of the world. And, when it was time to relax, the tensions were explosive. Because you didn't know whether you might live or die the next day, all the polite rules of behavior were shucked along with their fatigues and BVDs.

Ron: "I digress to my first influences being at those family reunions. My uncles were always into music. I recall I was around six or seven years old when I gravitated toward the musical side. There was a pair of twins that were on the radio every morning on the WLAY 1450 station serving the Florence/Muscle Shoals, Alabama, market. This was the Vandiver side of the family. They played music and I was lucky enough for them to include me. They taught me a few scores. Neither my brother nor sister was musically inclined. I was the only one out of our immediate family that was drawn to playing music. I did have cousins that were talented. As far as picking or what we called pickin', I was the only who that pursued it."

Due to its strategic location along the Tennessee River, Muscle Shoals played a key role in historic land disputes between Native Americans and Anglo-American settlers in the late 1700s and early 1800's. It was also the site of an attempted community development project by Henry Ford in 1922. Since the 1960's, the city has been known for music – developing the 'Muscle Shoals Sound'.

There are several explanations on how the city got its name. Some say the city gets its name from a former natural feature of the Tennessee River, namely a shallow zone where mussels were gathered. When the area was first settled, the distinct spelling "mussel" reference to a shellfish had not yet been fully adopted. Others say that the name comes from the bend of the Tennessee River around the area, the shape of which looks like someone flexing an arm muscle.

WLAY was one of the oldest broadcast radio stations in Alabama and the Southern United States. It had only aired music written and recorded in Muscle Shoals. The station signed on in 1933 as WNRA and has since secured its place in American music history thanks to its contribution to what is now commonly referred to as 'The Muscle Shoals Sound'.

Originating its broadcast as a variety format, WLAY was significant in its early years as a rare frequency that would broadcast both Southern Gospel and Country music and "race music" or music by African American artists. In the American Deep South, this was certainly unique. Several bluegrass and delta blues musicians made regular live appearances on the radio broadcast, including Bill Monroe, Earl Scruggs, Sonny Boy Williamson and Son House.

In the 1950's, WLAY balanced both country music and Rock and Roll music on its playlist. Sam Phillips, future founder of Sun Records, worked as a disc jockey at the radio station in his formative years and frequently cited the station's "open playlist" as the inspiration for what would become Sun Records in Memphis, Tennessee, blending both country and blues music to form Rock and Roll.

In the early 1960's, the station began to develop as a popular music capital in the United States and played an important role in its growth. Following the success of local resident Arthur Alexander and his hit single "You Better Move On", which was later covered by the Rolling Stones. The area quickly saw the rise of numerous recording studios. With this, WLAY became a meeting place for numerous Muscle Shoals musicians and songwriters as they would frequent the studios with new recordings. Percy Sledge's "When A Man Loves a Woman" was recorded at Norala Sound Studio by WLAY disc jockey, Quin Ivy and WLAY Chief Engineer, Paul Kelley. Kelley built Norala with equipment borrowed from WLAY's studios. The WLAY audience would frequently choose the "single" by artists such as Aretha Franklin, Wilson Pickett, Clarence Carter, and several others to be shipped nationwide after having heard the entire completed session on the air. It ceased transmitting in December 2014.

Ron: "The first instrument I learned to play was the guitar, an old Silvertone to be specific. Sears sold their very own brand, the Sears Silvertone guitar. It was a loaner. It wasn't the easiest to learn but through determination I persevered. If you play and your fingers hurt and bleed, then you consider yourself learning."

Silvertone was indeed the brand name used by Sears, Roebuck and Company for its line of sound equipment from 1915 to 1972. They were best known for being well-made yet inexpensive guitars, the brand becoming popular with novice musicians. Jerry Garcia, Chet Atkins, Bob Dylan, Tom Fogerty, Joan Jett, Brad Paisley, Joe Walsh and countless others had a Silvertone for their first electric, bass, or acoustic guitar. The Canadian band Chad Allan and The Silvertones, which would go on to become The Guess Who, took its name from this line of instruments.

Pete Townsend used them in a live performance with The Who for the purpose of smashing them after he'd played them. The guitars, especially the 1960s models, are frequently prized by collectors today. Two of the best-known Silvertone offerings are the Danelectro-built Silvertone 1448 and 1449, made in the early to mid-1960s. Today, Silvertone is a brand name used by Samick Music Corporation and was endorsed by Paul Stanley of KISS from 2003 to 2006.

Ron: "After the years passed, we would just go back and forth making trips to Texas. My dad, after serving twenty years in the Air Force, retired. I was in about the seventh grade when we moved to a town in Alabama called Leighton near Muscle Shoals. The most famous person from Leighton that I recall was the singer, Percy Sledge. The second most famous one had to be NBA basketball player Leon Douglas. He was Alabama's very first, first round NBA Draft pick, selected fourth overall by the Detroit Pistons in 1976.

Another notable was Ozzie Newsome, tight end for the Cleveland Browns, an inductee into the Pro Football Hall of Fame, and the current general manager of the Baltimore Ravens. Newsome played for the University of Alabama, where he started for all 4 years of his college career and he was nicknamed "The Wizard of Oz." Oh yeah, I am a Rolling Tide man through and through. These are, in my humble recollection, Leighton, Alabama's claims to fame.

As I graduated from that Silvertone, I learned to play the mandolin and the autoharp. Most are not familiar with the autoharp. The autoharp is like, I don't know, this thing you sit in your lap and has all these strings on it. You often see the Carter family playing it. June Carter played one and she was good at it too. Let me clarify. I played at it. I never really perfected it. The guitar remains my favorite instrument to play."

The autoharp is a trademark for a string instrument having a series of chord bars attached to dampers, which, when depressed, mute all the strings other than those that form the desired chord. Despite its name, the autoharp is not a harp at all, but a chorded zither. Autoharps have been used in the United States as bluegrass and folk instruments, perhaps most famously by Maybelle Carter, Sara Carter, Helen Carter and June Carter, all of the Carter Family. They are relatively easy to learn to play as a rhythm instrument but offer great rewards to the more committed player as a melody instrument. Grand Ole Opry star Cecil Null was the first to develop the upright style for playing the autoharp that was in turn used by the Carter Family. Maybelle Carter's granddaughter Carlene Carter frequently plays the autoharp onstage and on her recordings; her song "Me and the Wildwood Rose", a tribute to her grandmother, makes prominent use of the autoharp.

Ron: "Growing up we had high school bands we played in. When I attended high school if you could play the song, 'Stairway to Heaven', that's about the only song you would ever have to know how to play that really counted. You could play anywhere for anybody. One interesting story that occurred in my early twenties, 1978 or 1979, I, of course, also being an artist, which is really my first love, developed the skill using the air brush.

Back in the day air brush art was very popular. I would use it in a way, not necessarily on tee shirts, as is popular now. I used my skills to paint my artwork on banners. One thing led to another and there were a lot of bands in the area where we lived. These bands would cross over the state line to Leighton because we were so close to Tennessee where they would play at the clubs over in Etheridge and Lawrenceburg.

The way Muscle Shoals is logistically situated it is within forty miles of the Tennessee line and within sixty miles of the Mississippi line. It's kind of located in that corner. There wasn't a whole lot going on in Muscle Shoals because at the time it was a dry county. Of course, beer and music go extremely well together. Bands that were up and coming that were trying to make it would go to Tennessee to one of the wetter counties. This played more to their advantage,

Back to the air brushing, I met a guy that owned a western wear store. It was called the Golden Spur. Ralph May was the gentleman's name. Ralph had this knack for developing friendships with people that were not necessarily folks that lived in Nashville but were from Sheffield, Muscle Shoals and the Florence area, which they called Quad-city. People like Tammy Wynette, from

Red Bank, that very same area, and George Jones lived there during certain parts of the year. I developed this relationship with Ralph who owned the Golden Spur, and he would allow me once a month to go with him to fiddling conventions.

One fiddling convention that we went to a lot was Little Lin's Dude Ranch. She owned a farm and a dude ranch. She would have these shindigs twice a year. Ralph had converted this horse trailer over to a western wear store. I would set up right outside his trailer under a canopy and airbrush hats. Western hats were very popular then, brought on by singers like Mickey Gilley wearing those crazy hats with the feathers stuck in them. Those hats looked like a peacock on the front of them. Ralph developed friendships with these people. He knew them very well.

I was at home one night and it was about 10:30 or 11:00, late for sure. He contacted me and asked if I could come to the store. The store wasn't close to where we lived. Our house was on one side of the Tennessee River, and he lived on the other side. That's what separated Muscle Shoals from Florence. Of course, inquiring minds want to know so I asked him why he wanted me to come there so late. He told me that a lot of the guys that shopped with him don't necessarily want to come to the store during normal business hours. They feared being recognized and harassed. They preferred their privacy.

Ralph went on to explain that he had these three boys who needed a backdrop for their band. I said okay. What else could I say? At the time I kept canvas by the roll. I picked up a roll of it and loaded it along with my sign kit and headed there. When I arrived, and after introductions, I asked them the name of their band. They were called Bama Breeze. I said, let's think about it. I thought on it and came up with a design then painted Bama Breeze on it. They were satisfied with my design. I ended up gluing it to a window shade for ease so they could roll it up and then pull it back down. It worked perfectly. They were one of those typical bands playing in Tennessee or over in Mississippi.

A couple of months later I so happened to be in Ralph's store, in the back, doing regular work for him. He told me, 'Well I have some good news and I have some bad news. Bad news, Bama Breeze changed their name. Good news, they want another backdrop.' He asked me if I could design another backdrop for them. I said sure and asked what the new name for their band was. They had changed it to Wild Country. I said who in the world would name a band Wild Country? I went on to tell

Ralph that it was the stupidest name I had ever heard. Well, low and behold, the band members were in the store. Oops, they heard what I said. Not good for me with my potential redo now on the line.

The oldest band member told me it was a perfect name and that's what they are going to call it. He asked me why I thought it was stupid. I told them Wild Country sounded like an Avon cologne. Not to leave well enough along, I added, that as a matter of fact I thought it was one of their products, accusing them of getting the name from Avon. After our little debate they ended up keeping their name and I did the new backdrop. Low and behold, they went on to become the group, Alabama. From Bama Breeze to Wild Country and then Alabama…who could have known? There you go. I am famous for doing everything but an Alabama backdrop. They never commissioned me for the three-peat. Hard feelings...maybe."

    The band called Wild Country formed in 1969 in Fort Payne, Alabama when it had been founded by Randy Owen and his cousin Teddy Gentry. Owen was the lead vocalist and played rhythm guitar while Gentry played bass guitar and provided the background vocals. Their cousin Jeff Cook joined them, adding his musical talents on lead guitar, fiddle and keyboard. Operating under the name Wild Country, the group toured the Southeast bar circuit in the early 1970's and began writing original songs. The group became a professional band in 1972, adding drummer Bennett Vartanian. During this time, the group accepted a position playing at the nearby Canyonland theme park. In 1973 the band relocated to Myrtle Beach and became the house band for The Bowery. Working for tips, they played six nights a week honing the harmonies that would later become their trademark. They stayed seven summers at The Bowery, located fifty yards from the Atlantic Ocean, gaining a huge regional following. They changed the band name to Alabama, utilizing one drummer after another before Mark Herndon came into the picture. In July 1980, the band left their long-time gig at the Bowery near the Myrtle Beach Pavilion. They had changed their name to Alabama in 1977 and following the chart success of two singles, were approached by RCA Records for a record deal. The Bowery has been entertaining millions from all over the globe since 1944.

This portion of the interview with Ron is from June 2022.

Ron: "I was raised around music from the time I was eight years old. I never really connected with it until as an adult we returned home for the summer to Alabama. We would stay with my grandmother. That's when we attended the family reunions. Two of my uncles performed on the radio. They were twins. At the family reunions everyone wanted to play. All had a desire to be part of it. It resonated with me after we moved to Alabama while I was in middle school. My uncle would be wearing these fancy blouse shirts like Neil Diamond would wear. He wore a scarf with one of those shiny scarf rings. He was always dressed sharp. His car was sharp too. He always had plenty of '45' records. I remember him having a huge reel to reel machine for making recordings. I was too young to understand any of it though. He told me to come with him and he would show me. He took me to recording sessions warning me that I had to remain quiet. I would watch but still had no clue what was going on.

He recently reminded me again that my cousins were on the Grand Old

Opry. They were Rusty and Dusty. This would have been back in the Hank Williams days. They were a duo and probably a fill-in, but they had appeared on the Opry five times. We are somehow connected to the Vandiver's, from the same part of the country and settled in the same area of Tennessee, Virginia and Kentucky. The Vandiver's may have been some cousins twice removed, but it is a connection to music. Back then I was drawn more to the recording side rather than the urge to play. My uncle taught me to listen while he was recording the music on eight track recording. Each track is layered on top of each other. One track was guitar. One track was base. Each instrument or sound was on a different track often requiring them to be extremely creative when recording songs.

Muscle Shoals was the place everyone wanted to record. It is tough to fathom that he was the sound engineer that mixed these records for so many famous artists. After the session, it was critical to have the tape properly mixed before sending it to someplace like Nashville. When the Pickers started I always had the desire to record us, even go into one of the new studios they have now.

My dad was stationed in Mississippi for fifteen years in the Airforce. It was unheard of to stay that long at one location. As mentioned, it was after he retired that we moved to Alabama. As I became older, married and had children we grew apart. I was making tooled memorabilia using neon for soda bars, 50's style items. I met a gentleman who invited me to share a booth with him in Tupelo, Mississippi. I did, and at the time, my Trish was working for his furniture business, selling round beds. That's where she and I first met. She ended up going her way and I went mine. Later I was invited to visit Myrtle Beach one spring. Trish lived in Jonesville, Arkansas at the time. Her father was a professor at Arkansas State. I met her mom at the beach. Her mom has lived at the beach since 1989. I credit her with Trish and me reconnecting. We began dating and hanging out. I had already been married and had gone through a nasty divorce. I had no intentions of remarrying. I started a neon business at the beach. Well, she and I did marry. I had my business in Myrtle Beach from 1997 until 2006 when I sold it. I eventually landed at Coastal Carolina University, where I met Doug Bell.

North Alabama is well known for music. Rick Hall had a studio there from 1969 until 1947 recording some of the most famous artists. My uncle worked for Rick Hall in the Muscle Shoals Sound Studio. Etta James was one of the first people they recorded. Word got out to New York and L.A. about the quaint little town in Alabama with phenomenal sound quality. Mick Jagger heard about it and wanted to record *Brown Sugar* there. It was big news, but I didn't think much of it.

My uncle told me that they were going to pick up some clients at the airport. I was like, Muscle Shoals Airport? It was a place where only crop dusters used the runways. I was in middle school at the time. He asked if I wanted to go, and I went. It was at night. I was riding in the back seat. We arrived and a small jet landed. Back then you could pull your car right next to the plane. These guys exited the plane and got into a black limousine parked in front of us. They pulled away and my uncle asked me if I knew who they were. I didn't. He said that they were the Rolling Stones, here to record some songs in the studio. I was a kid, and it didn't really register me at the time what I was experiencing. Thinking back now, I could have gotten their autograph. I believe over eighty platinum albums were recorded in the tiny studio that had originally been a washeteria. My uncle saw it all as a sound engineer."

Ron continues, "George Jones lived in Muscle Shoals and would come home often, bringing Tammy Wynette with him. My dad owned an ENCO service station. My brother and I worked there, pumping gas and doing little odd and end chores. George would come in and I would pump gas for him. He came in one time riding a WWII motorcycle with a sidecar. He was drunk as a skunk wearing Snoopy googles and helmet. Ralph May, who owned that western store, introduced me to George and said he wanted a possum painted on his sidecar. He told George I could do it for him in an hour. I did it and he paid me with a one-hundred-dollar bill. I had never held a hundred-dollar bill before. I was proud of it and kept it inside my wallet for a long time and refused to cash it or spend it. George had autographed it. Looking back now I cannot believe I finally spent it. We later painted designs on buses for George and the Jones Boys.

I met Bill Monroe when he was at a fiddling convention at Loretta Lynn's place. I had met her husband, Doolittle, while peddling the western wear. He and George used to get drunk all the time. Doolittle wanted me to paint his wife's name on his stomach. I pushed back on painting Loretta on his belly. He then asked could I paint other things. I said, yeah. He then told me that Loretta wanted a painting of a mill located where an old bridge connected the entrance to the mill. He was drunk so I didn't think he would remember asking me.

Two weeks later Doolittle commissioned me to do the painting. I was in my twenties and had my oldest son with me when I delivered it. Loretta was home and invited us to have dinner with them, including her home cooked fried chicken. My son was like me when I saw the Rolling Stones. He didn't care. Being among celebrities didn't much impress him. We enjoyed the meal and Doolittle paid me with a check that had Loretta Lynn Enterprises on it. I didn't save it either. This was around the time that the *Coal Miner's Daughter* movie was filmed and launched in 1980.

Danny Singleton Journey

The following interview was conducted Christmas Eve 2015 during a family gathering at the author's home in Myrtle Beach. Danny is Gene Singleton's brother, married to Rhonda, my wife's daughter. Danny and his wife Karen attend most family gatherings. Danny Singleton met Ron Walker through his brother, Gene. Ron and Trish Walker's daughter Lexie attended school along with Gene and Rhonda Singleton's son, Winn at Carolina Forest in Conway. Both Lexi and Winn performed in the Carolina Forest Show Choir. Danny is a homegrown product, an original native of Horry County, S.C. He currently resides in his dad's house with wife Karen in Conway.

Horry, pronounced *Orr-ee* or *O'Ree*, was incorporated in 1801 with an estimated population of 550 at the time. Horry was surrounded by water back then, which forced those choosing to live there to survive virtually without any assistance from the outside world. The residents called their little community 'The Independent Republic of Horry.' The county was named after Peter Horry, a Revolutionary War hero born in the early 1740s. Over three hundred thousand now call Horry County their home. The county seat is Conway.

Conway is one of the oldest towns in South Carolina, originally named Kings Town by early English colonists and later changed to Kingston. Conway overlooks the Waccamaw River and is rich in history from the American Revolution. The Swamp Fox, Francis Marion, had an encampment near Kingston just across the Waccamaw River. After the war, patriotic citizens wanted to discard the name that honored Great Britain's King George II. It was originally called Conway Borough for

General Robert Conway but then in 1883, the General Assembly changed the name to Conway. Numerous buildings and structures located in Conway are on the National Register of Historic Places. One of them is the City Hall building, designed by Robert Mills, architect of the Washington Monument.

Some notable people born in Conway are Vanna Marie Rosich, better known as Vanna White of Wheel of Fortune fame. Professional golfer Kristy McPherson hailed from the area. Some may not know it, but McPherson suffered from Still's disease, a form of juvenile rheumatoid arthritis, diagnosed at age 11. Confined mostly to bed and unable to walk for a year, she was told she would no longer be able to compete in any sport that required jumping or running. She took up golf and played on the boys' golf team at her high school and the rest is history, so they say. Several professional football players originated from Conway; Allen Patrick chosen in the 7th round in 2008 to play for the Baltimore Ravens and Kenneth Earl "Junior" Hemingway, Jr. drafted by the Kansas City Chiefs in 2012.

    Danny Singleton recalls growing up in Conway. "The first memory I have of being interested in music was when I attended a church on Highway 544. I was just a little kid, maybe five or six, but I still remember Jeff Dunn's granddaddy, who is my mother's first cousin, coming to the church with his son and playing the gospel hymn, *How Great Thou Art*. That was the very first live performance I had ever seen. The experience and tune were quite awesome. The only singing up until then that I had ever heard were those songs playing on the radio. I was inspired to sing in the choir, but I didn't for years, not until the Lord finally came into my life. My life took many turns, but I said to myself that I was going to sing that tune one of these days. Well, the path has come full circle and I sing it now as a Picker. I have recently shared that story with Jeff Dunn, telling him, 'Look at me now. Here I am in your church performing, the place where it began for me.'

When Christ shall come
With a shout of acclamation
To take me home what joy shall fill my heart
Then I shall bow in humble adoration
And there proclaim my God how great thou art
Then sings my soul my savior God to thee
How great thou art
How great thou art
Then sings my soul my savior God to thee
How great thou art how great thou art.

  Did you know that this Christian hymn was based on a Swedish traditional melody and poem written by Carl Gustav Boberg in 1885? It was later translated into Geramna and then into Russian and became a hymn. It was finally translated into English by a missionary, Stuart K. Hine who tweaked it by adding two more verses. The composition was set to a Russian melody. It became popular during the Bill Graham crusades and is ranked second to most favorite hymn behind Amazing Grace. As Paul Harvey would say, 'Now you know the rest of the story.'

Danny: "My mother was sick a lot as I was coming up. I've lived in Conway most of my life, currently living in the very house my parents lived in and raised Gene and me. I lived in that very house until I was seventeen and ventured out on my own. I moved to Greenwood, S.C. for a while. Daddy was big on comedian Red Skelton and blue grass music. I followed in his footsteps and still am.

My great granddaddy was whittling a fiddle base and cut his leg with a knife. He got gangrene and they had to take off his leg. They say he was one heck of a fiddle player, so I guess music is in my genes. He later had Alzheimer's. Dementia is what they called it back then. My daddy would try to help him get around. That Alzheimer's would block out everything. They say he would forget about his missing leg and would somehow manage to walk everywhere. He was always into the music though. That seemed to resonate with people inflicted by the disease."

Danny reflects about life with his daddy. "Daddy's main job was working in construction. He sharpened saws on the side, making many a dollar sharpening those blades late at night out in the garage. A dollar was a lot of money back then. Everyone was bringing him their hand saws. He had earned a reputation as being the best around. He taught me to sharpen them when I was just a little boy. I was around eight or nine and would be on a construction site with him while mama was sick in the hospital. I spent much of the summer with him because of her illness. Daddy came up to me and told me, 'Take this drill bit and go over yonder and sharpen it for me.' I had never sharpened a drill bit before, but I told him, okay. I did the best I could and started sharpening it. Daddy elbowed one of his workers and told him, 'See, I told you even my eight-year-old boy can sharpen a drill bit', apparently making a point to his worker who couldn't. His point, the man was supposed to be a carpenter, yet he couldn't to this."

Danny, like Ron Walker, had a knack for being creative and being adept at using his hands, his talents, a correlation that, in an odd sort of way, connected both to music. Creativity can morph into many directions, music being one of them. While neither man knew the other, growing up separated by several state boundaries, the two were on a path with destiny. They didn't know it quite yet, but the Lord had a purpose in mind for them. Picking the pickers had a long way to go yet but the groundwork was being laid. It would be a firm foundation to build an everlasting friendship and camaraderie. *How Great Thou Art* was possibly the first hint of greater things to come.

Danny looks back on how he was a tinkerer at an early age, not yet drawn to the musical side but blessed with a gift just the same. "Daddy always had stuff in the garage. I was drawn to gadgets and figuring out what made them work. I would take things apart and then put them back together. I remember being at Greenwood High School on a construction site in 1969. They had all these locks that they called unit locks, left hand and right-hand versions, for the lockers. They could not be interchanged. There must have been three or four hundred of them. Fifty to a hundred of them wouldn't work so they were going to pack them up and send them back to the original manufacturer. Nobody there could do anything with them.

That attraction to gadgets overcame me so I commenced to messing with a few of the locks. I started taking them apart. It took me two weeks the first time in my spare time to try to figure them out. Now I was just seventeen years old, but I figured out how to take them apart and then put them back together using parts from left to a right one. Well daddy called them and told them there was no need to send the locks back that they had been changed and now worked. The manufacturer told daddy that it was impossible to interchange them. It can't be done. It won't work. They could not believe it because their engineers couldn't do it. Don't ever tell me something can't be done. They sent one of their guys from Indiana to Greenwood so that I could show them it could be done and how I had done it."

An artist, maybe not, but Danny had this gift to create or recreate, dismantle and reassemble, fix what had been deemed unfixable. His mind didn't work like most seventeen-year-olds. He envisioned other scenarios, looked at the world from a different perspective, determined to learn what made things tick. Think about Ron Walker, the banner maker, the hat designer, using his mind and his hands to create. Musicians are from that very same mold if you really think about it.

When had Danny really become interested in music? He claims he has always been interested in it. He had taken piano lessons for three years and he couldn't learn to play the way it was being taught to him. He said if they could have taught him in a different way, a way that he could connect to, that he might have stuck with it and learned a lot more. Danny explained that they tried to get him to do everything by the book, playing songs when he didn't know what they were supposed to sound like.

Danny explains: "When I got to the song, *Twinkle, Twinkle, Little Star*, I could play it because I had heard that tune before. I knew how it was supposed to sound. Other songs that they wanted me to play I had never heard before so that hampered me. My real handicap was the fact that I struggled with reading music back then. I couldn't remember all the musical symbols and notes. Reading the music and connecting the music to what it was supposed to sound like just didn't click with me.

I learned plenty of terms, but I still couldn't work the keyboard that well. I found that you could be awful a lot of different ways while attempting to play music, but, if you had the right timing, you could usually muddle through it. If the timing is off, you're done. I had learned the principles, but it didn't resonate to the application of playing.

At age eighteen, for whatever reason, I decided I wanted to buy my first guitar. How I got there from flunking piano is anyone's guess. A family tradition, maybe, but I'm not sure. Daddy always denied that he ever played a guitar. My uncle claims he had one and would play for them. He was quite accomplished until an accident that caused him to lose several fingers.

My uncle said daddy played all the time until then, but he would claim to me that he never did. I don't know why. One thing for sure, I never saw him play one.

When I had my first guitar, he had to check it out first. I could tell by the way he held it that this wasn't his first rodeo. Funny, for someone who professed he didn't play, he went with me and helped me pick out my first one. It was a Silverstone. Daddy suffered from PTSD. I think that impacted his thinking and the way he dealt with situations and with people."

PTSD is an anxiety disorder resulting from a traumatic incident in which flashbacks or unshakable thoughts about the trauma are common. Depression is characterized by an overwhelming and lingering sense of sadness and hopelessness. Symptoms can range from "feeling blue" to thoughts of suicide.

Well, well, well, does this sound familiar? The founding father picker first played a Silverstone. Could this be a sign or what? You can't make stuff like this up no matter how hard you try. Destiny, I tell you. Picking the pickers might just be a sign of divine intervention. Ah yes, there were powers working this angle for sure, a far piece to travel yet but destiny's road certainly lead toward Conway.

Danny: "It wasn't much of a problem deciding. The Silverstone only cost about thirty bucks back then. Eventually I would go on to buy a Martin. They made Martins like tanks back in the 70s. Now I have a Yamaha that is forty-two years old. I got the thing home after getting a good deal because the guy kept coming down on the price. He said it was his uncle's guitar and he wanted it to have a good home. He didn't want somebody to just buy it and resell it. He finally got down to just wanting a hundred dollars for it and it's probably worth two hundred or two fifty on the resale market. I wasn't interested in it at first because the strings were coming off it and coming unwound, but it still sounded good.

    I learned to play that Silverstone by being around other people playing and by attempting to read books about it. I basically self-taught myself. I just didn't have the attention span to do it by the book, like how I struggled with the piano. I couldn't connect the dots, that attention span thing. There were several things going on in my eighteen-year-old life. Probably the first four or five years I hardy played it at all. When I was about twenty-one, I met a guy from Keith Whitley's hometown in Kentucky. I bought the Martin from him. He was responsible for teaching me how to queue with a record. That sort of how I first finally connected the dots. Still, even then, I felt I could never progress and get to the point that I wanted it to be.

    I would jam a little bit with some guys, but I wasn't ready to be out in public doing any serious picking. I was that feller who just stayed back in the corner, trying not to mess up. I had some friends that were pretty good musicians. I would sit in with them. I never felt good enough to play in a band. About six or seven years ago, I met James Alexander Shelton who was lead guitar picker for Ralph Stanley for about twenty years. I had become friends with him on Facebook. He talked to me and encouraged me. Something in one of his videos clicked with me. I shared it with my brother Gene and my two nephews, Duncan and Winn. After thirty-five or forty years of attempting to play, often skipping four or five years, I would pick up the guitar and would see a little improvement.

Finally, I had someone that would take the time to pick with me. Wayne Brown in Abbeville, S.C. was that guy. He encouraged me to pick with him as had James earlier. A couple of years after meeting James, I began using some of his techniques; not actually copying him. He had advised me not to do like him. He knew how to tell and show people so that they could develop their own style; just use his way as a guideline. He said don't try to copy me because I make mistakes too. I guess it was three or four years ago, that I began to become satisfied with my picking. As part of the Pickers now, I am very satisfied with my picking."

Danny was asked if he played any other instruments.

Danny: "I took fiddle lessons once but those didn't go so well either. I tried picking up that fiddle again not too long ago and it felt like I was holding a tank.

I had bought some fiddles at yard sales. One of my highest moments was when I had just bought this specific fiddle and restrung it, then took it to Florence to resell it at the flea market. A black girl saw it and came up to me. She was learning how to play the violin at school. I had paid about thirty bucks for it. It probably cost about a hundred- brand new. I saw how she was so taken by it, so I sold it to her and didn't make a penny profit. She was so proud and excited that she would have her very own to play. That made me feel good, seeing how proud she was of it. She just couldn't thank me enough, that little girl jumping up and down for joy. I didn't make any money on my investment, but it didn't really matter because it was a nice little instrument for her."

How did you meet Ron Walker?

    Danny: "I met him through my brother, Gene. I got to know him better when helping build sets for plays at Carolina Forest High School. During small talk, I found out how multi-talented Ron was and that we both played. Ron invited me over to his house to pick. We would sit outside in his backyard around a bonfire and play the guitar. He mentioned that we ought to form a band, so I said. 'okay'. He calls what we do playing progressive music. Doug and I wanted to play the older stuff." (Doug Bell would eventually become the third picker but Danny had not yet met him.)

Danny recalled the first place that they ever performed in public. It was Conway Manor, a nursing home in Conway, that provides patients with skilled nursing care as well as private or shared accommodations. This would become a recurring theme for the Pickers. They enjoyed playing at such venues, bringing heartfelt joy while uplifting those unable to take care of themselves or venture into the world they had left behind. A greater calling, a transitional period would develop, one that would most assuredly define the emerging Horry County Pickers and their purpose, that divine intervention thing again.

Danny with nursing home friend.

He reminisced about the very first time that he played in front of people. "We played at Conway Manor. Funny, I guess this was something I always really wanted to do. I was nervous, maybe had a few butterflies, but I wasn't afraid. The more we did it, the more comfortable I became. Now I thoroughly enjoy it, being in front of a crowd, butterflies gone. I have even learned to tell a few jokes, simple ones, not ones with lengthy innuendos, to lighten things up. I like to tell ones like the one that a guy went for a job interview and the interviewer asks the first question. I want to know what you consider as your worst fault. The guy replies, my honesty. The interviewer repeats, your honesty? He says yes. The interviewer says I would think honesty would be a virtue, not an impediment. He said I don't care what you think."

Danny doing what he loved doing.

Did anything memorable happen, one for the blooper reel, at Conway Manor, this being the first gig? Not a blooper by a long shot...

Danny: "Tommy Holt, now a resident, was raised right around the corner from me. He had a birth defect which impacted his ability to walk. I had always helped him with his wheelchair. He almost leapt from the wheelchair, hugging me. We reminisced about old times. He told me that he appreciated how I stuck up for him when others gave him a hard time. He came from a poor family, not uncommon around these parts. I never made fun of him. I'd always greet him, hey Tommy, how are you doing, treat him the same as anybody. It's funny what we remember.

Sometimes what seems so little can be so large. He was always such a good-hearted soul for a man disabled his entire life. He had ended up at Conway Manor, like so many. His family had already passed before him leaving only a brother who could no long care for him at home. He had lost one of his brothers at a local motel, a girl shooting him over a teenage argument. We performed twice there before Tommy passed away. Seeing him and hearing this was worth it to me, going there. I will never forget Tommy Holt".

Then there was Brookhaven.

Danny: "We played at another assisted living home, Brookhaven. This one lady there said the next time we came we would have to play nude. You must smile and nod your head when things like this happen. We went back but we kept our clothes on for the performance. The residents had voted on who they wanted to have play their annual reunion and we were selected. They fed us and paid us for that one. It was the first time we had ever been paid to perform. We always volunteered to play, proud to uplift those confined. The people at Woodhaven are so nice and appreciative.

Most of the residence at Woodhaven want to hear the old stuff like tunes from Roy Accuf or Hank Williams. Some of the staff like us to play John Denver songs like *Rocky Top*. Now *Rocky Top* is a well-recognized and beautiful song and a lot of fun to play, but I feel our band will be remembered for playing Roy Acuff songs instead of John Denver. Everybody and their brother played *Rocky Top*. I want us to be different, stand out and not be like everybody else out there. Most of these folks in the nursing homes really appreciate the old stuff. We focus on playing these venues because we enjoy doing it for them and for us. There is this one lady at Conway Manor that knows the words to every song we sing. Music is the common leveler."

Sometimes an experience can take an unexpected twist. Such was the case as another story evolved, one from a visit at Conway Manor. The Pickers choose to play these venues at no charge. It's just what they do, what they enjoy doing. Giving back to their community warms their hearts. Typically, they go with the flow but sometimes the flow passes through turbulent waters. This is one of those situations you never want to find yourself in the middle of, and when you do, you get through it the best you can.

Danny: "We were at Conway Manor. A gentleman, a volunteer, had a Sunday worship service there. Like us, he was giving back, even plays a little guitar during his service. I think this was our second visit. We set up the equipment and began playing. This guy came up to us and asked if it would be okay if his wife got up there with us and sang a song with us. Of course, it was fine with us. She wanted us to play *I'll Fly Away*. He said she was a great singer. So, we start, and the guy walks over to Ron playing the guitar, without asking, grabs Ron's banjo. You know, most musicians are funny about just anyone using their instruments, especially without asking permission. Ron, being the gentleman, gave him an odd look but didn't confront him.

After the song, another guy comes up and tells us, 'By the way, next time you come, it is going to be different. They told us we can no longer have our Sunday morning worship service here so the time you are here on Saturday is our new allotted time. You can only play the songs designated by us, what I deem appropriate for the service.' He went from nice to bossy in the blink of an eye. Ron, trying to keep the peace, asked him what he wanted the Pickers to play, thinking the gentleman was a resident. He suggested songs that we had not practiced and got angry when we couldn't play them. We had no choice but to do our set, songs we did know. As only the Pickers can do, they worked through the uncomfortable situation the best they could and didn't make a scene."

The Horry County Pickers traveled to Due West, S.C. to the Renaissance Retirement Community as a personal favor to me. This was a five hour drive from Conway, but the guys didn't blink when asked. I had a book signing there and they were having a seasonal festival, crafts and other goodies being sold. The Pickers were a hit. Many of the residence joined in singing and dancing. Our grandson, Winn Singleton, sang with the trio making it a memorable event. The Pickers commented that this was the first time that they had ever had dancers. Thank you, my dear friend, Ann Grubb for your contributed vocals and thank you, Susan Jackson, for your hospitality. Gary Wiles, a local legend from Abbeville joined them. An entertainer always travels with his instrument of choice and his was in his vehicle. Gary plays with a band every Thursday evening at Lowndesville, South Carolina. He blended in perfectly with the Pickers. He, too, often travels to the Renaissance Retirement Community to entertain the fine folks there.

Renaissance Retirement Community Performance

(Doug Bell, Ron Walker, Gary Wiles and Danny Singleton)

Renaissance Retirement Community Performance

T. Allen Winn, Winn Singleton, Doug, Ron, Gary Wiles and Danny

The Pickers have also played at the Grapefull Sister's Vineyard in Tabor City, North Carolina, performing at the first annual Alzheimer's event and others that followed. As always, their appearances are strictly volunteer. Again, I was there promoting books, all vendors donating a percentage of their earnings for the cause. We thank our gracious hosts Amy and Sheila, the vineyard owners.

The Horry County Pickers had the honor of playing at the Conway Riverfest. This was Danny's first real public appearance, singing in front of a large crowd. A friend in the crowd yelled, 'You need to tell them who you are!' They had forgotten to introduce themselves, too taken by the crowd. Sometimes Danny travels to Shallotte, North Carolina, saying that the venue there welcomes strangers to perform. Danny's passion is playing bluegrass. He mentioned that a gentleman travels from Laurinburg, N.C. once a month to do workshops in the area and teach those who are interested in learning bluegrass music. Danny thought more should do what they can to pass on the trade to others.

Danny said another influence on him was Ronald Singleton, his daddy's first cousin, a member of the local bluegrass society. He was one of the first three-finger banjo pickers in Horry County. Though a small handful of other banjo players had dabbled in similar styles, the most popular kind of "three-finger picking" was first popularized by Earl Scruggs while Scruggs was playing for Bill Monroe. Most banjo players at the time used styles that included strumming the strings with the back of the fingernails, on the second half of each beat.

Scruggs replaced that strum with a single note picked upward, which gave him more flexibility in playing melodies. Since he no longer had to rotate his wrist to play the strum, he could "nail" his pinky and ring finger to the banjo head next to the bridge and pick at lightning speeds with his thumb, index, and middle finger only. This is the heart of "three-finger picking." It also took the banjo from being mostly an accompaniment instrument to being a lead instrument. Danny added that he didn't often have the chance to see Ronald play except when he appeared on local television. Channel 3 out of Wilmington featured these shows. He recalled another bluegrass favorite, the Red White Family, having seen them perform in Aynor.

Danny: "I guess my most favorite and most humbling place that we've played up until now must be the First United Methodist Church at Fantasy Harbor. We were on the big stage with a packed house. We were on stage with singers and a couple of dancing horses that used to perform at Dolly Pardon's Dixie Stampede. A guy told me that you should never share the stage with animals. I told him that Doug and Ron aren't that bad. The reason for the advice, they'll always remember the animals but won't remember you."

Where does Danny envision this journey continuing?

Danny: "I personally would love to go up to Holden Beach, North Carolina. They have a bluegrass festival there. They have some great pickers performing there and they tend to welcome newcomers. It's a far piece from here to travel though. I haven't quite convinced Ron and Doug into going yet. I'd even settle for us playing in Shallotte. In all fairness, it is tough driving there and arriving by 6:30 or 7:00 when Ron and Doug work until 5 PM. I'm retired so it's a bit easier for me. I have friends who play there frequently. The name of their band is 'The Grass Needs Mowing.' They are a progressive band. Shallotte has always been a laid-back town. Anyone who has an instrument is welcome to take turns at the microphone, what they call a round robin of picking or playing.

I would never want to play at the Bluegrass festival at the convention center. That's just not one of my ambitions. At one time when they first started out, the atmosphere was much different. If I had been picking thirty years ago, times were different, and I might have wanted to play there then. Not now, it's become too huge and is not open to just anybody."

Ron, besides picking and being musically inclined, is also an artist. Danny is very creative too, welding and building various unique items. How does yours overlap into music or does it?

Danny: "I really don't have that artistic depth that Ron has. My creations take forever. Ron and I were talking just the other day and I reminded him about the time how he came up with this idea where he needed to get down to a screw in the bottom of an air conditioner and didn't have the correct tool for the job. He proceeded to take a screwdriver, a bit, a wrench, pair of pliers, duct tape and a piece of string to construct a mechanism to assist. He kept messing with it until he removed the screw. I tried the same thing with my brother, Gene, and we ended up looking like a couple of idiots.

I recall another time when we were starting on a show and my picker clip needed repairing. I pulled out my versatile pliers and said here's my tool kit. Ron goes and grabs a paperclip and fixes it, the whole while I was telling him it wasn't going to work. I told him that the difference between him and me is that I wasn't taught perseverance. I come up with ideas but don't follow through with them. I have good ideas, but he has ideas and makes them work. I give up too easily.

I blame my daddy for me being like that. He was a little bit that way too. Some things he would never quit on then other times he would try for a while then just up and quit if it didn't work right to suit him. It was the PTSD again. I remember one time he was contracted to build this brick wall and it didn't matter that it was quitting time. He had decided he was going to finish that wall and he literally worked eighteen hours straight."

Did your daddy ever hear you pick?

Danny: "Yeah, he made a remark that I could hardly hit a lick until buying that Martin guitar. A Martin is the Holy Grail in bluegrass music. He made that comment sometime before he passed and I'm ten times better now than I was then. I felt extremely proud when he paid me that compliment. He was extremely short when it came to praise. I'll have to confess, I had it rough mentally, coming up with him. I would like to say that my daddy taught me how to make a living, but he never taught me how to make money. You had to do it just the way he did it. Don't ever go to work for another company. You were supposed to stick it out with the same company, and you were never supposed to start your own business. He would tell me, you're going to fail, you're going to fail. He never offered any advice to help me chose my path. Instead, he just belittled me every chance he got.

He had a way of beating you down. He always made fun of things I was trying to do. When I tried a project on my own, he would make fun of it, telling me he had more important things to do than watch what I was doing. He would just laugh and treat it as nothing. Flipside, when he would be on a job and become mentally impaired due to pressures, he would seek me out to go there for him until he recovered. Sometimes it bothered him that my salary was coming out of the budget for a job. Like I was supposed to be free labor. Funny, it wasn't even money out of his pocket, it was budgeted for the company's project. His policy was that he might not ever finish a building on time but when he walked away, he walked away from it leaving it in good shape. He didn't have to go back and fix anything.

It was tough living with him. I became quite rebellious at times. Sometimes, I would just have to leave. We probably spent four or five years apart, where we didn't see one another at all. Something came up and he called the people in Greenwood where I was working and told them that I was doing stuff unethical on the job. That was a lie, just his way to get me fired and come back home. It was always something job related between him and me. He told one place where I was employed that I was letting a guy working for me intentionally mess up the doors and all sorts of stuff that was not true. I'd had enough and I called him. I told him I was the one doing that job. Stop telling stories. I told him to go to hell. I didn't want to see him again.

    He treated my brother, Gene, the same way. Back then I had convinced myself that he treated him a little better but, looking back now, I don't think he really did. I remember this one time I wanted to install a shower in the tub and Daddy wouldn't let me, claiming a shower would rot out the bathroom floor. That was how he was with me. My ideas were never good enough. I wanted a stereo and didn't get one for the same reasons, my idea and wrong. I was never really the jealous type growing up. I worked side by side with guys, some making more, others making less. It really didn't matter to me as long as I got mine."

Danny retired from a life driving eighteen wheelers. How had it gone from construction to that job choice?

Danny: "All I had ever done was work seven days a week without ever having a vacation. The only way I would get a vacation with Daddy is just stay out a couple of days. He would track me down and make me go back to work. I was living in Greenwood and my construction job had run out. I had to go on unemployment. I think that was the first vacation I ever had.

I learned to weld while out of work, getting on one of the programs they offered. I'd go back to work for a few weeks, working not stop and then be out of work again. I finally decided to try something different and went to truck driving school. It seems I was never attracted to higher education until I reached forty years of age and then wanted to go all the time. I got my license and drove trucks for fourteen years. I logged in a million miles. I would sometimes be gone seven or eight weeks at a time. I lived a life of not making a lot of money, but I did what I wanted to do.

While on the road I did carry a guitar with me a good bit of the time. I had an old Conn guitar. Conn was not highly regarded as a guitar maker even though they were better known for brass instruments. It didn't sound that great but was a nice guitar at one time. It was at the very low-end price of a Martin, about four hundred and fifty dollars back in 1974. They had a better reputation for manufacturing trumpets. After a few short years the Conn's sound got worse and worse. I finally gave up on it and stored it underneath an old shed. I think a piece had broken on it. My friend Wayne Brown found it and asked about it. He wanted to work on it and replace the new strings. I told him to have at it. That thing didn't mean much to me one way or the other. Wayne did just that. He fixed it. He had it sounding like a five-thousand-dollar instrument.

Wayne is an accomplished guitar player and enjoyed playing it. Sadly, it started coming apart again. He told me that he was going to place some stove bolts in the bridge and restring it. Guess what, when he finished, it still sounded good. Next, it started caving in. Wayne put a stick in it, and it still sounded good. I could have spent three or four hundred dollars on that darn guitar, and I would still have had a fifty-dollar guitar. I'm glad Wayne got use out of it. It sure didn't have any sentimental value to me. I also gave away that old Silverstone years ago to somebody who helped me clean out my apartment. I was never attached to hardly any of these instruments. I reckon not being that accomplished had a lot to do with my decisions.

When I was eight years old Daddy told me that Bill Monroe was going to be playing at the Myrtle Beach Pavilion. Of course, I had never seen Bill Monroe and I thought he was going to take me. Typical Daddy, he follows up telling me he wasn't interested in going to see him. Not to be outdone, I told him I had saved up my allowance and asked him to take me there. I didn't care whether he went to see him or not. Imagine that. He took me and dropped me off. I walked up to booth at eight-years old and bought my own ticket to watch Bill Monroe.

When I got inside there was a whole bunch of kinfolks there, Singletons older than me. I often wondered if Daddy knew they were going. Was that why he let me go alone? My Uncle Albert was one of them. He had always been good to me. The Pavilion was known for top notch entertainment in its heyday. You couldn't believe everything Daddy told you. He said Stonewall Jackson made his first appearance there. That was before my time. I guess you could Google it now and find out. I really didn't get to go see very many shows there. Daddy didn't do stuff like that when we were growing up."

Danny reflects about growing up in Conway. He recalled a conversation he and Doug Bell once had about how Conway used to be back in their youth.

Danny: "Conway was always clannish. I remarked to Doug that if we had known one another growing up that we couldn't have been friends. We both knew why. Back in the day if you weren't raised in the town limits of or didn't go to the grammar school you could never be in the society clique. The town kids would ostracize you if you were from the country. Don't think about going into one of their mama and daddy's stores because you would be ignored. They wouldn't even wait on you. The black people got treated better than us back then. My first cousin's mother carried him to school every day to avoid awkward situations. It was tough growing up in the sixties in Conway.

Doug lived in town and his folks had a farm too. It was tough because he couldn't bring his farm friends around his own friends. They wouldn't mix. Doug's family moved to West Virginia for a couple of years. Doug said they didn't have that problem there. Everybody was treated as equals. He said that was the happiest two years of his childhood. I had cousins that wouldn't walk down the halls of school with me because it was unacceptable. You could walk in the backdoor with them but not in the front door. Away from school they treated me fine.

Daddy always built me up to be as good as the 'so called' upper crust and not to hide from it, to hold my head up high. I tried to fit in where I could, but it was a tough row to hoe. I was even on the honor society. Even that didn't matter to those that felt they were the only ones that did matter. I finally had my fill. I realized that I didn't fit in and wasn't learning anything. Out the door I went. That was the tenth grade. I was reading on a college level, but it didn't really matter to anybody but me.

I love reading. I average reading three hundred books a year. I used to read anything and everything. I guess, as I have gotten older, I now just want to read something entertaining, novels, funny subject matter. I can't read history like my brother Gene. I get too bogged down in it. I guess my hobby, if you want to call it that, is being a mister fix-it. I enjoy helping people when I can. When I leave this world, I hope those who knew me remember me as being the nice guy.

Daddy was always known as being the meanest man around. I want to be the opposite of him. I wish I had his perseverance though, his tenacity to not let something go until finishing it. He once put this brick wall in the wrong place before he realized his error. He spent all day taking it down and putting it back up in the right place, never telling anyone he had made the mistake. He made very few mistakes and he didn't want anyone to know he had made such a huge one. Perseverance was indeed his mantra."

Daniel Keith 'Danny' Singleton, age 70, died September 1, 2021, at the Conway Medical Center after a long illness. As Danny said, he loved working with his hands. Quite the adventurer, in his early life he even worked on a shrimp boat. Too bad he is not around to share the many stories he had about that experience. Besides construction work and driving an eighteen-wheeler, he operated those large, towering cranes for a spell. There was not much he couldn't do when he set his mind on giving it a try.

Once he mastered those musical instruments and had made it to retirement, his passion was playing bluegrass for churches, local festivals or any place where people loved and enjoyed a picking session. One of his favorite places was The Gospel Barn. He possessed a quick wit and had a gift for storytelling. He enjoyed telling a good joke and would laugh even if those listening didn't. He had a distinctive laugh to boot.

> IN LOVING MEMORY OF
>
> DANIEL (DANNY) KEITH SINGLETON
>
> JAN. 21, 1951 † SEPT. 1, 2021
>
> OH COME, ANGEL BAND
> COME AND AROUND ME STAND
> OH, BEAR ME AWAY ON YOUR SNOW-WHITE WINGS
> TO MY IMMORTAL HOME

Doug Bell Journey

Doug bookended by friend Vickie and his mother

This interview of the final Picker was conducted June 28, 2022, at the author's home.

Doug grew up in town but spent a lot of time with his grandparents in the country. Because he spent so much time in the country, he identified with the country folk more so than those living in town. Danny had shared stories about being slighted because he was considered a country boy, not a city boy. Cultures in Horry County tended to clash a bit.

When Doug was young, his dad ran a general store in the Homewood section of Horry County. His dad played music all day long every day in that store on a record player located on a shelf. He always played honkytonk music from the 50s, favorites being Kitty Wells, Webb Pierce, Faron Young and Hank Williams. Doug hated that music. He preferred classical music when he was in his teens. He still listens to a lot of classical music. Doug played the trumpet in the junior high band and while in high school took violin lessons for two years. He had taken piano when he was younger but admitted that he had never gotten anywhere on the piano.

In his sophomore year of college, 1980, then nineteen-year-old Doug, came home for spring break and ventured to the Conway Library. While checking out the usual classical music records he spotted a record titled *Country Music, South and West*. For some reason he was drawn to the artwork on the cover, so he selected it and brought it home too. The LP included two songs by the original Carter Family. As soon as he heard them begin playing *Gospel Ship* he was hooked and credits it for changing his life. Doug became obsessed with the Carter Family music. That led him to old time music that had been recorded in the 20s and 30s. When he heard the Carters singing, he remembered the music played in country churches that he grew up in. He had attended those churches with his grandparents in the early 60s and had heard that music many times.

Doug went into depth explaining the origin of the music and the notes as depicted on sheet music. He explained that the music notes in these old gospel song books are either rectangle and triangle or filled in black or not filled in. This form of music was developed in rural Spartanburg, South Carolina in the 1830's. Better explained, it was four-part harmony sung in those old churches. He could still hear remnants of it from his childhood. He sat in the old people section with his grandparents and could hear that old timey sound. That rush of memories returned when he heard the Carter Family singing. It's called a flashback for a reason.

When Doug returned to college, he borrowed a guitar from a boy down the hallway that was hardly ever used by him. He began practicing on it. Upon returning home, he discovered another instrument to advance his playing. Doug's mother's brother (his uncle) died at the age of fourteen in 1937. He had owned a Sears Roebuck Supertone guitar. It had been stored in a trunk since 1937 until 1969 at his grandmother's when she gave it to him. It had been at his house, but he never had the desire to mess with it. Now, he found a reason to retrieve it. Between his college buddy's guitar and his uncle's, he self-taught himself to play. He explained that the Carter Family only used three chords. He learned those chords. He played everything in C, F and G.

Doug was now on a quest to find Carter Family albums and began rummaging through secondhand and junk stores for the treasures. He now has quite the collection. Ron suggested that Doug should change his middle initials to 'LP' because of all the 33s he owns. That song, *Gospel Ship* had set the hook. He learned listening to the records, how to do the Carter Family lick on his guitar or so he thought, but what Maybelle Carter did was much more intricate than what he learned. Maybelle had the ability to play the melody with her thumb and the rhythm with her finger. Doug admitted it was very complicated and took more coordination than he possessed to pull it off. During this span, Doug was basically a closet musician. He might occasionally play in front of family, but it was rare. Doug had no musical family influences.

After Doug began listening to the Carter Family, he also started listening to others from that era like the Blue Sky Boys and Monroe Brother. He never quite latched onto contemporary bluegrass back then, other than his admiration for Bill Monroe. He gravitated to the older style country music, and ironically found himself falling in love with that junk his dad used to play in his store. Things had come full circle, possibly unknowingly brainwashed as a kid.

Doug claimed he didn't develop much, finding himself in ruts and just remaining there. He was drawn to the mandolin when he was twenty years old but never got one. Fast forward thirty years when he bought his mandolin. He said he believed in deferred gratification. As bad as he wanted a mandolin, he never touched one during that thirty-year span. He finally bought one from Mister Chestnut who owned a music store in Conway. He still remembers him as being tall and thin possessing a little beard, a very talkative gentleman. Mister Chestnut made the instruments and was well known for his workmanship. He was a philosopher and a good old man according to Doug. Doug often visited his store to converse with him. Knowing his love for the Carters, Chestnut contributed Carter albums to Doug's collection.

Chestnut had a gentle way of talking. Doug told him he was thinking about taking the plunge and purchasing a mandolin. He added that he may not be able to play it and wanted to start by owning a cheap one. He could not afford Chestnut's handmade versions and needed to find an 'old something'. Chestnut didn't have any 'old somethings'. He told Doug, 'You want to find an instrument that is quality because of the pleasure you will get out of it whether you learn to play it or not. You need a decent instrument.' He finally suggested one that he had in his shop and Doug bit the bullet and bought it. It wasn't one he had made. It was a Michael Kelly brand. Chestnut professed it to be a quality instrument and that Doug would enjoy playing it. He did and said he will never own another one because he fell in love with that one. Modestly, Doug claimed he isn't that good and is incapable of doing fast runs. He admits he can at least trill and manage the melody. He is not interested in buying another instrument. He added that if he could really 'smoke it', he might be interested in purchasing something else. For now, he is content.

Time for the instrument count, just how many does Doug own? He acknowledged that he played guitar all those years but never bought one. The 1937 Sears Roebuck was gifted. He only borrowed his college pal's so that one doesn't count. His mother-in-law had a boarder one time, and when he moved out, he left his guitar. Doug ended up with yet another freebee. He had never purchased a guitar, only his mandolin. He still has his violin from high school. His high school band trumpet is in the attic. The final instrument tally is five.

Doug said he had a bad musical experience while in the fourth grade. Everyone in the fourth grade had to take tonette and learn how to play it. The tonette is a small, end-blown vessel flute made of plastic. The teacher would pass them out to everyone in to play then she retrieved them before class was over. No one was allowed to take them home and practice. Doug never got the hang of the tonette. All year he just pantomimed, pretended to play it. He was terrified of it.

His parents split up when he was twelve and his mother moved them to West Virginia to live with an aunt and uncle for two ears. It was there that he learned to play the trumpet in the band and was quite good at it. He loved it. The trumpet remained in the attic until about six months ago when Doug thought he would give it another whirl. His lips would no longer form the puckering, blowing technique to produce the sound required to achieve trumpet excellence. Back to the attic it went. Ron was disappointed, telling

Doug they could have incorporated the trumpet into a routine to utilize when performing at Mexican restaurants.

  Sometimes Doug wakes up terrified, thinking about singing in public. He perceives himself as a terrible singer. He added that one thing about old timey music was that the people were not great singers. He had never sung in public until his debut with The Horry County Pickers. They had sung in practice only with Danny and Ron cattle prodding him to launch his career in the public arena. It was a terrifying hurdle to overcome for all the Pickers. Ron claims that a charity event at the Grapefull Sister's Vineyard in Tabor City ranked as the scariest time because they performed with a seasoned local artist, Paul Grimshaw and his band. Paul possessed an impressive song book that looked three inches thick and he never looked at it while playing. This made Doug nervous as well, unlike playing at the nursing homes where the audience wasn't particular and were usually very forgiving.

They have also played at the area adult daycare center, more folks that appreciate their talent or at least overlook their faults. Doug said his family seemed to enjoy his performances too. Reflecting on the Carters, he said they had a unique quality and never considered themselves showmen. In another life, Doug could have been an honorary Carter Family member.

Ron interrupted during the Doug interview stating, 'I am going to reveal something I have never shared. Before Doug's last birthday and before Danny's passing, I attempted to book a turn to perform at the Carter Family Fold. I am on a two-year waiting list.'

Doug shocked, asked, 'When are we going?'

The venue located in Hiltons, Virginia is open for concerts and performers. It is preserved for old time country and bluegrass music. Performing there would be a bucket list item come true for the Carter Family fanatic. Doug had attended the 75th anniversary event there commemorating the Carter Family around the 2003 timeframe but performing there would be epic.

Doug modestly admits he has no aspirations beyond being content with what they are doing. He again said he is not a great public performer but, as bad as he sings, he can usually sing without forgetting the words and reasonably on key. He can do rhythm all right but added that in public when he does a solo performance on his mandolin, he often messes up. Would the average person even know it? 'Yes, they would,' said Doug. He compares his abilities to the character, Asa, on the Andy Griffith Show. Asa is the night watchman at the bank. When he pulls out his gun, it falls to pieces. Doug claims that personifies him when he begins to perform a mandolin break. It just falls to pieces. His ultimate goal is for his breaks to be solid. When asked how you work on something like that, Doug said he didn't know, adding that they are fine when he does them at home and in practice. All bets are off when he performs in public though. He becomes Asa. He doesn't struggle with it at nursing homes but if they perform at something like a festival or a venue where they get paid, look out. It must be psychological.

For two years, Doug and friend, Jerry Long, did a radio show in Loris, S.C., WLSC station. The show aired on Friday mornings called 'Down at the Barbershop.' They were tasked with playing old timey music consisting of a set of four or five songs. He claimed all that practice and he never got better at it. He added that he messed up every week for two years. Doug laughs saying he expected to get a pink slip while playing at the radio station. Danny Singleton played with them a few times on the radio show. Jerry's dad was mayor of Conway for years. The Long family has a 'long' history in Conway. The Jay Rueben Long Detention Center in Horry Count is named after a family member. Jerry heads up a current band that Ron and Doug play with, The Picadilloes. Jerry was a Rolling Stones fan in is younger days and liked the Blues as well.

The Danny Singleton Tribute

**Oh come, Angel Band
Come and around me stand
Oh, bear me away on
Your snow-white wings
To my immortal home.**

The surviving pickers (Ron and Doug) met at the author's home June 28, 2022, to complete a book project that began Christmas eve 2015 that had fallen by the wayside. On that Christmas Eve at a family gathering, the author had conducted interviews with Danny and Ron chronicling their personal journeys. In June of 2022, Ron had posted an iconic photo of the Horry County Pickers on Facebook a few days earlier prompting open dialogue between Ron and T. Allen Winn. It led them to finishing the book project, feeling they owed it to Danny to close the chapter and publish it. What you are about to read is T. Allen with Ron and Doug, over sandwiches and desert, as they pay tribute to the memory of Danny Singleton, sharing favorite stories and Danny-isms. Then the Pickers later picked Danny's favorites in what turned out to be a four-hour session that night. (Videos of them picking and singing are posted on the author's Facebook page @ T. Allen Winn, dated June 28.)

Doug, Danny and Ron

Doug is still amazed at what a big reader Danny was. They were asked what they miss most about Danny.

    Doug: "His personality, his big heart, always smiling. He always had a joke."

    Ron: "That was his part. He told jokes during the performances. He was the joke man and storyteller of the group. I miss his disposition on life. Danny had a knack for lighting up a room. If you were serious, you wouldn't be serious for long around him."

The two pickers pondered some Danny-isms.

Doug: "Danny enjoyed eating. They visited restaurants frequently with Danny and wife Karen."

Ron laughs, pointing to a knot on one of his fingers. "Danny called it a calcium deposit. He told me, 'I can tell you how to get rid of that, Ron. WD-40 is good for everything, that an axle grease. Spray some WD-40 on it and then hit it with a hammer, it will break up and it will dissolve into your body. It will be gone.' I have never mustered up the notion to do what he said. WD-40 and a hammer, the perfect Danny-ism, will fix anything that ails you."

Doug: "Danny had the mind and spirit of an artist."

Ron: "He was a creative person. He was a phenomenal metal artist. He could make metal yard art. He would get hung up on one thing for a while before moving on to something else. He could make anything from something I would have never thought of. Danny could take a flywheel, a garden hoe, a gear and a piece of rebar and make an artsy person out of them. He was uniquely artistic."

Doug: "He made a statement with his clothing too. He sported colorful shirts with his overalls. He wore some of the wildest shirts."

Ron: "He was wearing a new pair of overalls and I asked him, 'Do you not own an old pair?' He said, 'Sure I do but we're going to town.' I can think back on my grandfather, and he did the same thing. He wore his old overalls around the house but when he went to town, he put on a new shirt and overalls. Danny aways said he was living the Carter Family lyrics *the sunny side of life*. I will never forget how Danny played a big part in moving my daughter Lexi several times in Cincinnati. It would be just me and him. While there, I took him to a place called Gabriel Brothers. It's a store that sells seconds. He found a pair of brown Carhartt overalls for twenty dollars. He could not believe they were just twenty dollars. He then went right over to the Hawaiian shirt rack to match one to wear with them. Hawaiian shirt with overalls, quite the fashion statement and trailblazing trend setter he was. He accessorized his outfits with a train engineer hat."

Doug: "He looked like Boxcar Willy wearing that hat."

Ron: "A visit to Danny's yard was a unique experience. It was a mixture of a salvage company, Goodwill and a Pick and Pull auto parts junkyard. It was a very complete yard if you needed anything. Like that sawblade I needed, he had it. He had an uncanny ability to locate anything he needed, a method to the messy madness. With his artistic outlook and ability, he was freer than any one of us. I mean that with all my heart. I wish my mind and heart could have been as free as his was. We all worry about things that never crossed Danny's mind. He really didn't care."

Doug, "My wife and I visited Karen after Danny died and a doorknob on one of the doors was a pair of vice grips."

Ron: "There was probably something wrong with the doorknob and he clamped it on there as a temporary fix. It worked just as good as the doorknob, so he never replaced it. Plus, it was just another extension of his artistry. Why would you want anything else if it still opened the door? You could open and close the door and lock it at the same time with a pair of vice grips. That was his explanation. You almost laugh but then he stops you in your tracks and you must think about it."

Doug: "Danny loved drinking coffee."

Ron: "He owned the biggest coffee mug I have ever seen in my life. It looked like a half gallon jug with a handle. He drank coffee all day long. Coffee to him was like a person with a cigarette unable to work without one hanging from the corner of their mouth. He worked well if had his coffee. It made him think better."

Doug: "Danny was always interested in his heritage. His ancestors were members of Hebron United Methodist Church on Buckfield Road. It is an extremely historic church. We played there one cold Sunday morning. It is supposed to be the oldest church in Horry County. Danny told me a wonderful story about his great grandfather's generation when they all rode in wagons and congregated at the church for a picnic or event. Anyone who had tiny babies, they would let them sleep in the back of the wagons. Some of his kinfolk supposedly switched all the babies to different wagons. As only Danny could tell it, every family went home with a different baby. Danny doesn't believe they ever got all of them straightened back out to the original parents. That was one of my favorite Danny stories."

Doug: "Danny loved telling jokes, but I couldn't understand any of them.

We never did a show where he didn't tell a joke. It was to humor what Salvador Dali was to art. Lost in translation!"

Ron: "There was no stopping him. We were better off letting him go because he was so bent on what he believed in and what he was going to do that you basically just followed his act if you wanted peace. He would see the jokes online or he would just make one up. He always wanted to make a statement. It might be political or nonpolitical. Most were extremely political. Doug was always terrified that Danny would tell the wrong kind of joke in front of an audience. We warned him to keep politics out of the performances and Danny would ask, "Why."

Doug: "Most of his jokes during performances were not political or maybe I just couldn't understand them.

Most people must have gotten them because they laughed. On stage he kept a straight face when telling one. When just around us he would laugh while telling the joke."

Ron, "Most made absolutely no sense. There would be a preacher, a dog and a mailman and they went to school together and then they got out for recess and did something. He would be laughing at whatever the punchline was supposed to be. That was his freedom that I mentioned earlier. I wish I was that free, not one to worry about what people might say or hear. Danny was his own person. That's what I call freedom, buddy."

Doug: "Every time I said goodbye and left him, I always left with a good feeling."

Ron: "I must tell this story. We were blessed to have met a woman who played with the Long Bay Symphony. She played the violin, very well trained. We had to have sheet music for her for everything we played. She had always wanted to play in a bluegrass band. We invited her over and she was phenomenal. I still have the video of her auditioning with us. She could make you melt away.

Danny would always rush things. He said, 'Thank God we got a fiddle player.' I told him, no, she hasn't made her mind up yet. She had only played with us a couple of sessions at my house. In his mind, we needed a fiddle player. He asked her, 'Are you in or out?' She had survived an abusive past, so this tone didn't sit well with her. She was shy around guys because of the abuse she had endured. We wanted to make her feel welcome. Danny wanted an answer and would settle for nothing less. He texted her numerous times wanting that answer. She never returned to play with us. This was a Danny-ism for sure."

Doug: "Danny could find someone anywhere he went, the laundry mat, a doghouse, people that were interested in playing with our group a time or two."

Ron: "He was our agent. We went to Shallotte, North Carolina one time and Danny knew all kinds of people there. He always wanted us to perform there. He invited us to play at a senior center in Shallotte. We loaded all the equipment and arrived at the place. It was shut down. We said nobody was going to play that night. Those Danny-isms came out of his mouth then and he said, 'The hell with the both of you, I am going over to the gazebo and play in the public park.' That's where we went."

Doug: "A bunch of people that Danny knew had showed up to jam.

Everyone proceeded to set up in that gazebo. It was in the middle of July and blazing hot. We played for two hours. It was one of the best times I have ever had. My hands were cramping up. Lot of people showed up to watch. Danny had a way about him that might make you mad, but it would not last long."

Doug: "We returned to a nursing home because they had enjoyed our previous visit. We were performing a Hank William's song *Hey Good Looking*. A man walked up and said, 'This is a religious service. You are not going to play any music like that.' Danny found the microphone, spoke up, 'Now look here, you didn't tell us that and we are going to play what we planned to play."

Ron: "Me and Doug looked at one another. It didn't lead to a fist fight, so that was good."

Doug: "I think the guy was a family member of a resident and had never seen us perform. We do play a lot of religious songs too but not everything we play is that genre."

Ron: "You often hear that people with Alzheimer's relate to music and tend to remember every word. I will never forget that time after time there would be people in attendance that couldn't speak but would perk up when we played. One lady was fidgeting with the tablecloth with her fingers but as soon as we began playing a couple of the religious songs she stopped. She began mouthing the words. Danny, in his heart, realized this about the people in these facilities. He had a soft spot for the elderly. He had a big heart for those sheltered and unable to get out and about. I believe his tough upbringing impacted how he emotionally felt about it."

Doug: "Danny befriended people everywhere he went. Our bass player who still plays with us, moved here from Virginia. Danny was the first person he met after relocating here. They became great friends."

Ron: "Danny was always proud to introduce you to someone he knew. Many had something to do with music.

Ron: "One of Danny's favorite songs that we will be picking tonight is *White Dove*. Doug's wife tagged this song as The Picker's song on our social media site. There's another one of his favorites, a sad song about a mill closing, *Aragon Mill*. He enjoyed singing that song. Danny loved *Angel Band* and *Sing me Back Home*. I have begun to write a song about Danny, more poetry right now, no melody yet. It's titled *Labor on Blue Collar Son*."

Ron's Tribute: *Labor on Blue Collar Son*

*No need for a map
To tell him where to go.
Don't need for a guide.
To tell you where the river flows.*

*Lace-up boots and faded overalls
A homemade sandwich, a half jug of old joe.
Behind the scenes, below the grade
Hardly noticed but part of everything.*

*Labor on my blue-collar son
now that your work on earth is done.
You're flying high where you can run
Labor on my blue-collar son.*

*He's got a mind of his own
and changes it, when he wants.
A self-made man with a choice,
plain and simple he's just one of the boys.*

Labor on m blue-collar son

*now that your work on earth is done.
You're flying high where you can run
Labor on my blue-collar son.*

*There's really nothing that he can't fix
up his sleeves are many old tricks.
His hands may be rough and hard,
His overalls might be plain,
But his heart of gold
Is without a stain.*

Labor on my blue-collar son
now that your work on earth is done
You're flying high where you run
Labor on my blue-collar son

Doug: "Danny had health problems, but it wasn't like he had a decline. The last time I saw him was not too different from the first time I saw him. When you lose someone like that, it is almost like you can't believe they didn't make it. He used to come to the radio station in Loris and play with us a lot. He was experiencing his throat issue back then. He got back to playing and practicing with us regularly. He would come to my house and practice sometimes.

One of the last times he was there, Karen had dropped him off and went to Belk, not too far from where I live in Conway. The battery in her car died and I went there and jumped her car off. This might have been the last time I saw him before he landed in the hospital. He called me later that week to tell me he had covid. He wasn't feeling well and ended up in the hospital with covid related pneumonia."

Ron: "I was in the Conway hospital about the same time with covid also. I was admitted and remained there for two days. I had an infusion that brought me out of it."

Doug began perusing his text exchanges with Danny around that time period.

8/12/21 Doug: *Danny, how are getting along?* Danny: *I'm doing good. I think I only have a cold. That can give you a positive test result. I have had colds a lot worse than this. Hope you and the missus are doing good. I hope I will be doing well enough to attend on the 20th.*

8/19 Danny now in hospital. Doug: *How are you doing today?* Danny: *Doing better since they got me into a real hospital room last night. I was in a cramped treatment room until someone got discharged. Doctor said I need to gain some weight back. Thanks for checking.* Doug: *Hope you can get your weight back so we can be out picking.* Danny: *I am missing it big time.*

8/23 Doug: *Danny, how are you getting along?* Danny: *I just can't get my oxygen up. The x-rays are good. Just out of breath.* Doug: *We are praying that you will get your wind back and feel better. I heard from Ron this morning. He has covid. It's going around.* Danny: *Sorry to hear about Ron.* (This was the last text exchange Doug had with Danny.

Ron peruses his text messages too.

8/30 Ron: *How is it going Danny?*
Danny: *Not good. Bad oxygen levels. My spirits are staying up. How are you?*
Ron: *I was admitted for covid.*

8/31 Ron: *How are you doing?*
Danny: *Not good. Bad shape. I am so weak.*

Ron: "Danny was always optimistic. This was the first phone call that he wasn't."

Danny lost his battle September 1st.

Doug: "I received a phone call on the first of September from his wife, Karen, at 10:42 to tell me he had died."

Ron: "Danny had a series of issues beginning with his heart being out of rhythm, then the covid related pneumonia. I think everything, including covid, had played havoc on his system."

If Danny was sitting across the table from you two right now, what would you like to say to him?

Ron: "First I would want him to go pick. That's the way he would always open up. I would tell him that he has been an inspiration to me."

Doug: "I would want to tell him that I am glad I got to know him. He enriched my life. I hope he kind of knew that. I know he was thrilled and took pride in when we started picking. He heard that sound that he liked."

Ron: "We still play it in the same style that we did when he would sing songs. We use the same runs."

Doug: "Danny had a special way of picking. He cross picked and did little runs, old timey country sounding runs, beautiful."

Ron: "And he would always say, 'Ron, just do this right here, pointing out the note sequence to play, saying every other one, every other one. This is simple, Ron. You can learn it.' He told me the same thing at least three hundred times. Nope, I never got it right"

Doug: "I'm good at rhythm and can do some melody playing. While I was chopping, he would be doing rhythm, back up picking while we were singing."

Ron: "Danny got us into bluegrass."

Doug: "It was Danny's main type of music. He knew the music backward and forward. He also knew all the background about the music, all the musicians, the songs, everything. He told me one time that he had seen Bill

Monroe perform during the fifties at the Myrtle Beach Pavilion."

I recapped this very episode as told to me by Danny. Ron nor Doug had ever heard the backdrop to the story, Danny's dad refusing to take him to see Monroe and instead dropping him off at the ticket booth to go inside alone. Danny's dad could be cruel as Danny offered many examples of his cruelty.

Ron: "Any time a disagreement would come up, usually it could be resolved by him saying he had never had anyone to come back at him. I would say I hate you feel that way. Tell me why you feel that way. It would give him a chance to voice his opinion. I think that voicing his opinion was important to him because, damned if you do, damned if you don't, he is going to get his point across. Once he made his point, he would settle down and listen to reason. The cruelty inflicted by his dad had given him low self-esteem issues."

Doug: "Danny was once a long-distance trucker."

Ron: "He wore a lot of different hats and knew everything about whatever hat he wore. He was not a jack of all trades. He was an expert on them."

Ron: "Danny would be so excited when he bought a vehicle or traded for a vehicle. I will never forget when he bought the white Explorer and the truck he bought for pulling his welder. He was so proud of that Explorer. It was a used vehicle but to him it was a new car. Who cares, it was new to him. He came to my house driving it. Danny had this way about him. He didn't jump out of the car saying come here I want to show you my car. He held back, wanting me to say, oh my gosh, where did you get that? Once I acknowledge that, he said, 'Oh, I just picked it up. Let me tell you all about it.' Danny then basically verbalized the manual telling me every bell and whistle that it had. He insisted I sit inside while he showed me everything. Then he asked if I wanted to take a ride in it because he said it drove like a dream. He was a man of vehicles. He owned so many. The only vehicle that he never drove was a gold Ford Fairlane that has been parked in his yard forever. There is also a 1961 truck there."

I interrupted Ron to tell him that the 1961 Apache 10 Chevy truck belonged to my papa. I ended up selling it to Gene, Danny's bother, just before we moved to the beach in 2005. I had no place to keep the truck. It was the toughest thing I had ever done, letting that truck go. I had been given the truck in 1988 when my papa could no longer drive it. He passed in 1990 at the age of ninety. I never had the heart to go out to the property to look at the truck since living here because it pained me terribly that I had let it go.

Ron: "Danny tells the story about that truck and what it meant to him, his brother Gene and Duncan (Gene's older son). They began fixing it up when Gene wasn't too busy with work. Danny spoke of the precious times when the three of them would tinker with the truck. That was a favorite time for Danny."

T. Allen Winn's Papa's Truck

The Horry County Pickers are no longer the group they once were but pickin' remains in their blood. Danny will never be forgotten. The memories were stronger than ever that night in my living room as they played many of Danny's favorites, remembering how it was when the three jammed and picked for the love of it. Ron Walker, Danny Singleton and Doug Bell, forever the acclaimed Horry County Pickers.

Daniel Keith Singleton

January 21, 1951 - September 1, 2021

"But as for me and my household, we will serve the Lord."

About the Author T. Allen Winn

Winn began writing in 2003 while being cooped up in hotels during business travel. Completing a 650 page so called novel he became hooked. The homegrown Abbeville, South Carolina boy embraced the experience completing one novel and then leaping into the next one, fun and therapy at the time. That changed in 2011 when a chance encounter brought stranger and new neighbor Bob O'Brien to his Pawley's Island doorsteps. Bob did not realize the neighborhood home had been sold and apologized when Tom greeted him instead of the man he had expected to see. Book in hand, Bob had just published his first novel, The Toppled Pawn and explained the previous neighbor had shown interest in writing. Tom remarked he dabbled in writing to which Bob asked, do you have a manuscript? Tom replied 'ten'. Bob had just started Prose Press, a publishing company and suggested publishing one. You cannot make this stuff up.

T. Allen Winn's first novel, Road Rage joined the ranks of the published a few months later, and he owes a special thanks to Bob O'Brien for making this possible. His first seven books were published by Prose Press. In 2016, T. Allen Winn established Buttermilk Books, his publishing company and has now published thirty-five books. He and his wife reside in Myrtle Beach, South Carolina.

Ole 'T' does not write a specific genre. He writes what strikes his fancy. If you don't see something that fits your reading wheelhouse, just tell him what you like, and he might just write it for you.

Books are available on Amazon or online where books are sold. Select books are available at Southern Succotash on Washington Street in Abbeville, S.C., in Tabor City, N.C. at Grapefull Sisters Vineyard, and at Calabash Art and Curios in Calabash, S.C. Or *Message* T. Allen Winn on Facebook to arrange delivery of signed copies, or to schedule him to speak at an event or book club.

Fiction from T. Allen Winn

The Perfect Spook House
Dark Thirty
Lou Who
Raw Ride, a Wild West Zombie Apocalyptic Shoot'um Up
The Man Who Met the Mouse

Mister Twix Mystery, a Cat Scene Investigation
Come Here, Getouttahere, Tyler's Tail Wagging Tale
The Tenth Elemental
Last Stand on the Grand Strand
The Lord's Last Acres
Covert 19, 2020 A Devil of a Year
The Sot and The Savior
Outside the Clique
Guns and Ashes, Four Friends at a Fish Fry
Forced Family Fun, God Bless the Whiteside's

The Detective Trudy Wagner series

Road Rage
North of the Border
Tithes and Offerings
Trudy Wagner, Southern Belle, the Prequel to Road Rage

Bigfoot Trilogy

Book 1: Foot, Tree Knockers and Rock Throwers
Book 2: Another Foot, What Really Happened to D.B. Cooper
Book 3: Final Foot, Willow Creek

Non-Fiction from T. Allen Winn

Being Bentley, A Dog Like No Other
December's Darkest Day, While I Breathe, I Hope
The Hardwood Walker of Port Harrelson Road
Cuz, My Brother, Life is Good, God is Good
The Horry County Pickers

Memoirs

The Caregiver's Son, Outside the Window Looking In
Vol 1: Cornbread and Buttermilk
Vol 2: Don't Sit Naked in a Grits Tree
Pushed Into the Pull, Thank You Cuz
The Endless Mulligan, Short Shots from the Golf Whomper

Books with Co-Author Benji Greeson Abbeville, South Carolina Football

It's All About the 'A'
It's All About the Angels in the Backfield

Biographies

Clay Page, Somewhere In Between
Screw It, Let's Ride, The Legend Bub Lollis

www.ingramcontent.com/pod-product-compliance
Lightning Source LLC
Chambersburg PA
CBHW060322050426
42449CB00011B/2613